THE BOOK OF YOU AND I

WOLFWITHINK

Made with love on the Notion Press Platform
www.notionpress.com

PLAYLIST

1. Have we met Before
~Sarah Barrios, Eric Nam
2. 8 Letters
3. Strawberries & Cigarettes
~Troye Sivan
4. Wonderland
~Taylor Swift
5. Snow on the Beach
~Taylor swift
6. How you get the Girl
~Taylor swift
7. Must have been the wind
~Alec Benjamin
8. Criminal
~Britney Spears
9. Overdrive
~Conan Gray
10. ILU
*~Elijah Woods***11. 24/7 365**
~Elijah Woods
12. Angel Baby
~Troye Sivan
13. Perfect
~Ed Sheeran
14. Until I found You
~Stephen Sanchez

To, Kevin Hayrle

(the root of the tree
from where a
flower blossomed)

f o r e v e r

if the time was made of colour
you'd be my golden hour
i'll take the batteries out of my clocks,
and whisper wishes from far below
we'll be stuck inside this moment
as if time is stopped
in a sea of strangers
lost in reverie, a world so serene
a touch of velvet, a feel of a gentle breeze
the scent of roses, the taste of sweet wine
i'll restart my clock, begin the time
and know that <u>we are infinite</u>
<u>in the book of You and I</u>

dear diary

i met somebody, he smelt of *unlit cigarettes* it was ***nostalgia*** as we reached for the same book and his hands brushed over mine, I've heard in nostalgia there's no difference in a day, a year or decade, or a lifetime. because the amount of longing is beyond the idea of time. *I felt love not by the brown hue of his hair or his clothes, but his eyes earthed me. Not the moon's reflection in his eyes but how he gazed at it.*

sometimes having a shelter is a luxury, but now **I have a home**, isn't that more luxurious? I saw flowers growing from my ribs and making a playlist. we went to a museum together but the **only muse I was listening was him, my heart had 71 beats that minute.**

as friends obviously. <3

his sweet voice wrapped over me and made my being humane, maybe I have read too many novels to confuse this with love. i fell in it. not to drown but to dig, dig and find what? *Perhaps a part of me he stole from starsss*

to, the angel.

i wonder if the
heavens know that
an angel has been
missing since we
met

crimson red bedsheets pleasant ballet sounds
by two birds in love outside
heavenly happiness
like van gogh art or yellow colour

you're the metaphor which is rich to my poetry
like ancient folklore fall effortlessly
heartful smell coming from his collar
hugging handwritten letters
attached with roses

I'm the string, you're the violin
you're a moon landing on earth
soon my body will be buried
but *I'll wish you love*
even after my next birth.

why i want you to be happy?
It's like asking the sky why is it blue
or like why do birds sing, or why does
the sea has endless waves
your smile gives me peace.
if someday, the stars that shine for short time
you fade into depth of darkness
my sky would miss your spark and glow

all the time.

<3

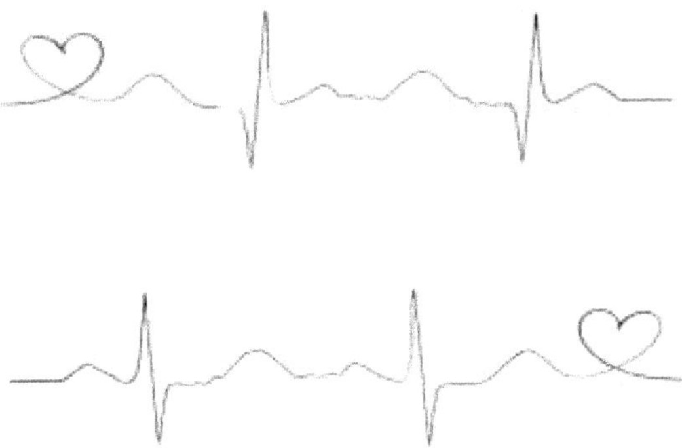

my coffee stained lips
your soft mellow hair
our wrinkled white sheets
and melon scented air

staring at the moonlight
wind wafting through windows

you smile, i smile, exquisite.

and **forever** in our eyes

your hands tangled with mine
my head on your head
our heart beating a soothing rhyme.

and our paths entwined

all these words
i've painted you in
every canvas
the only label
every art
the only muse
my book is a museum of you

— your heart, my faith.
your mind, my religion.

please be happy

breathe. everything will be okay.
your eyes say how many times you've tasted the pain
i know it feels unbearable, but it will pass
you survived it then, you can survive it now
keep breathing again and again,
i promise this will pass.

I know there are haunted memories
inside your ribcage
but if you show me your teardrops
i'll collect them like rain
because you're too precious to cry

you have stars behind your each eyelid
and the entire universe in your soul
so be all right, it will pass
as long as you're holding my hand

if you're heaven
i would love to die
if you're pain
i would love to get hurt
if you're tears
i would love to cry
if you're moon
i'll be the closest star
if you're the pollen
i'm the flower
if you're ocean
i'll be the wave
if you're a chalk
i'm the blackboard
if you're the paper
i'm the pen
if you're the drawing
i'm the artist
if you're the muse
i'm the writer
if you're the night
then i'm the dream
and if you're the dream
then i'm forever asleep

when i'm with you,
there's everything in
nothing.
and when you're not
there,
i feel nothing in
everything.

— the smell of
your perfume

no blanket is as warm
no pillow is as resting
no bed is as comforting
as being with you <3

I woke up with *lilies* in my sheets.
I heard tales of love and glory in novels and wondered what it's like to fall.
all the things that fall they break then why the people are so eager to conquer

i heard whoever dealt with it got themselves burnt

what is it?

it begins with a **knot in the chest, an aesthetic ache and heaviness that scribbles poetries inside out veins,** the neurons take it to the heart which gets a motivation to beat faster every minute it transfers ***this love*** till the entire body and reaches the **DNA**.

how do I know this? **because of you. <3**
Haha they say *you can't love someone until you don't love yourself.* but I still see black in my eyes and I've never seen a rainbow hue in someone's voice.

there's no pink in my roses, there's just hue of all the sunsets we have spent together. there's no storm in my heart there's a nostalgic peace. a calmness which makes me feel safe. I've never hoped for forever because it's different for everybody practically. for an ant a forever could be few months. for a butterfly a forever could be 5 weeks. for humans, 80-90 years. **I just know you're a part of my journey that'll be the core of me. the version of me in every life might sing your melodies. your name could be the echo when somebody stands on my grave and**

~~Ps: (Looks like I'll say everything apart from ily fowget pleesh >~<)~~

you make
me realise
that “love”
is a verb.

we are paper hearts
floating through moonlights
and dancing till midnight
until it *rains* and we *melt*

I remember the night
we stayed up past 4am
once I told you I wake up at four
and you were there at the sharp
all time I kept thinking that night that
I could listen to you forever

that was the moment I fell in love
*red heart × infinite*

Time and distance can't separate us
for what we have is so real

— ily

you always keep questioning yourself
"do I deserve this, what did I do to deserve this"

haha, just know, in any version of reality in a hundred lifetimes or in a hundred worlds.
you're enough. and everything about will always remain enough.
pinkiest promise.

i think of you so *constantly*, **every word i write, the air I breathe, the blood that runs through my veins.**
you're inseparable

if love is rain
you are the storm
my favourite storm

"i love you" doesn't mean
I'll stay
that's why I don't say often

count the *grains of the sand* and
leaves on a tree or the *stars in the sky*, or *the beauty of nature*, or the
water in the ocean.
Even their number is not
enough to define the time

— please stay alive and smile.
always. every time. forever.
constantly. lifetime. day and night.
repeatedly. endlessly. <3

don't think you don't matter

someone always wonders if you're okay
someone smiles on thinking of you
someone hears songs and think of you
someone prays for you
someone feels comfortable with you
someone feels the happiest on seeing
you happy
someone cares for your presence
someone loves you
<u>you matter the most.</u>

- *my breath*

you're my muse
and I'm your artist
so let me carve you in
every rhyme
for my love for you is
infinite

— I've fallen so deep, but I
feel so free

Sun and Moon

the theory says that
there are infinite number of universes
and in those infinite number of
universes
there are infinite number of ways
we could have *met and fallen apart*
even the most carefully planted seeds
cannot flourish where they're meant to
stay
but have you ever heard,
<u>sun and moon never dies</u>

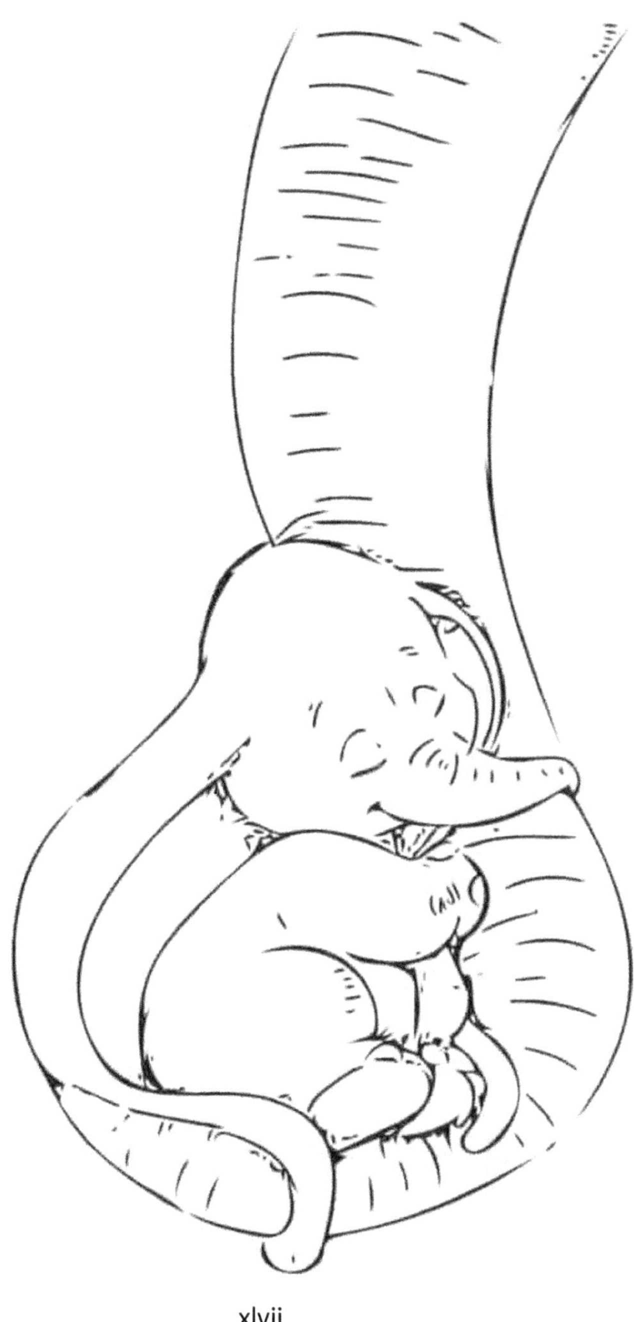

broken roads
maps unknown
mud house or igloos
quaint towns or zoos
no matter where we go
our paths entwined
will **forever** feel like **home**

<3

falling for you was *poetry*, I don't know which form but it came so naturally just like breathing.

our language is as old as the stars. all these constellation in my hair speak your tale. a person who looks like a *forever.* of **your eyes that consume horizons and elegance that made meteors come down to earth to witness your glory.**

— the moon landed on earth for you. **you're the real moon. <3**

h a y r l e a n d w o l f

Eclipse of Heart

make me feel things that i don't
understand,
when we gaze at the crystals
hanging on an *invisible thread.*
and how we dream
that we someday would be sitting on it
for rest all the days,

but we live our lives misunderstood,
I don't know why it feels so good.
I've been wondering about you and I
stars and skies, fate and time,
say you and i, it's such a crime
'cause you're killing me by the most
beautiful sign (drum beat haha)

every star tells me what we can be.
every night makes me fall into dreams,
ringing bells of the autumn air
brown hued, the sunset sails
leaving brush of loving trails
now even the stars are blinking in the skies
dinosaurs are chirping, are we stuck in a dream or this is the *verity of life*

once upon a time
without an intention or a rhyme
maybe I fell for a falling star
wish I would have known it from the start.

"*and they lived happily ever after*," she ended with a thin smile.

"*but mother, does that mean for the whole rest of their life? how's that possible?*"

"*well, there's no way to find it, princess. but some eyes are worth falling for*," her dad looked at her mother with a smirk.

daughter smiled like a candy, "*good night, mom. good night, dad*."

as they both covered her with the blanket and, gave her a kiss on the forehead.

PLATFORM 9 3/4

i walk into the crowded world like a
normal day,
busy streets and busy souls on my way.
forever is a lie when you walk into them,
every memory of ours is meant to be
hidden.
you passed me over, our eyes were an
accident
i stepped in the train, before i could
explain
how would i tell you that my forever has
come again?

is it only me who feels this way?

you got the eyes that once i had fallen
for.
is it the soul for whom i would stay?
oh, we've been here before
i don't know why, but i wanna die to
follow you

take me home, and tie us again
where we would sit and i'd sing songs for
you,
with the guitar on my hands in the
borders,
platform nine and three quarters.

purple silky sky caresses,
blueish cotton candy clouds,
beneath the falling leaves and glitters,
oxytocin of red heartbeats beating loud.

remembering the days when we
checked
the mail box which looked a little so
lame,
how we kept waiting and waiting for the

hogwarts letter that never came.

now as the silvery stars illuminate
the shore of trains

as the amber leaves of birds sleep
and the lavender magic smiles so sweet
as the unicorns chase the black and grey
running through the oceans deep.

it dusts the wand
and the truth of past life is revealed.

as i fell into your eyes, i was pulled into
this scene,
irises coloured like a deep chocolate
we could never find a magical wand but
yet the *time and space got paralyzed*
and the universe we had never known
how we dwelled in there still and called
it paradise
there was a man standing in the
everglow
i was crying in the dark looking for you.

he said “what lights you up is what you
should own.” and dumbledore asked
me "are you sure?"
i broke my wand, making you my last
wish
as i let go of my magic for the sake of
love like this.
you fell down from the divine
enchantment,
for me, that moment, time had been
frozen
'cause i knew *i loved you more than any
magical wand*
dumbledore smiled at me and we woke
up as muggles as i wanted it to be the
present.
and finally, the train gets stopped on the
platform.

she walks by,
as he is looking at her eyes once again

of a colour unknown to him
black grey rough sky brushes
as the rain starts pouring in heavy
sounds

beneath the falling stars and witches
the pain of his broken wand bleeding
around

pale skin, chalk white faced man with a snake and a cat with red eyes came out of the train

following the traces of the guy and the girl left. He had the look in his face, and unicorn blood in his soul that everyone in the Hogwarts were familiar with.

He was following her, hoping she might remember him. in the middle of the crowd, in the middle of the walk, she felt the breath of a dragon. All at once, she turned back and looked at the man, and it was someone that she had known in the back of her mind *"you are..."* As soon as she noticed, he turned back with a deep whisper, "VoLdeMoRt'"

before she could say anything to him, The man's skeleton-like body turned back with, his heavy nostrils, he took out his greyish white wand as he pointed it towards the rainy sky while breathing in his strident voice "astraferina cassiopeiadum!"

the broken wand on the sand suddenly glittered as he ran and she stared.

"astraferina cassiopeiadum" is the spell that aligns stars.

The Moon told the Stars about us

it was the story, i fell for a star;
the soul that had no face, made no pace.
wine after wine, the sky aged like my skin,
i longed every night to be under its light.

last night i heard the curse of death,
blood on the floor, the wolves were crying.
i was looking at the moon helplessly,
it shed its tears at me.
life after life, the sky aged like my skin,
in no life I could find my love,
not even the star i followed.
the moon gave me empty words to swallow.

i beared everyone's death; i couldn't breath
my *sword* had *sinned,*
my *soul* was *stitched.*
the moon counted the nights
i waited for your return.

for once i wanted to be cast in the sun,
for you, i'd look at the sky until i burn.

poisonous tears run down my face
love is death; as death is you.
i used to dream; i used to pray
to the shooting stars
now, I'm so high in this;
feels like I can almost shoot a star

sky had no stars, land had no men,
tombs were empty, but my heart had you
love perished souls away
like the shells on the shore
it was you and me, all alone my soulmate
that was left to vanish for someone else's fate.

one day, you will be no more
the sky will be painted by stars
of happy endings and fallen souls
but i never want to die
i never want to die
if it's not for you.

"*Don't you think it's time to let go?*"

"***look at the sky***"

"*It's like the stars are vanishing with the souls. Earth is almost empty*"

"***but i can still see, that one star, shining so bright*" ****smiles****

"*Mm... one of them is mine, right?*"

"***You're that star. Look into your eyes. No star is brighter*" ****smiles***

"*how on earth someone like you can exist?*" **smiles back*

"***its not me. it's just love. and it exists because you exist*" ****smiles again***

"cannnnnnnn I getttttttt a kisssssssss"

"kissessss"

If I am the
poet
You are the
poem.

the sands of time engulfed by sea
I'm confused to which chapter are we
So before I met you
I thought love was *pretty pathetic*
poetry for a poet
you made me a poet

your spirit is so calm and wild
watercolour blue skies
I love to breath in this
your beautiful eyes
maple syrup air
orange blend
shiny dust
and you. <3

Little things which are not so Little

Dark winter nights / 2am talks / lost in music / the taste of chocolates and ice creams / sharing about our day / moons and stars / Peace / smiles and laughs / kisses and sparks / butterflies and sparrows / Taylor Swift and Olivia Rodrigo / cats and fishes / Tom and jerry / cartoons and Harry potter / Titanic / Santa Clause / poetries and you. <3

-

-

I want to make your wounds scars

I'll stitch all your atoms through mine

the universe always
has a plan for you.

you're santa's gift
<33

we are a *hierarchy of pulses*
merged together into a disorder
I've never known such a peace
almost how the sky crawls up
its way to the moon

- unmapped cosmology

you're

the

closest

thing

to

magic

I just want you to be happy always

....

....

....

.... *<3*

www.ingramcontent.com/pod-product-compliance
Lightning Source LLC
LaVergne TN
LVHW021143160826
845679LV00023B/2029

9798889757641